Living Desiderata

Applying Its Poetic
Wisdom to Our Chaotic Times

Francis Williams

Living Desiderata
Applying Its Poetic Wisdom to Our Chaotic Times

© 2025 Francis Williams

This book is an independent work of analysis and reflection inspired by *Desiderata*, the public domain poem written by Max Ehrmann in 1927. The interpretations and insights presented are the author's own and are not affiliated with or endorsed by the original author's estate.

While every effort has been made to ensure the accuracy of the information provided, the author and publisher make no representations or warranties regarding the completeness, reliability, or suitability of the content. The material is intended for informational and inspirational purposes only and should not be considered professional advice. Readers are encouraged to use their own discretion when applying any concepts discussed.

Edition Information:

First Edition: 2025
ISBN 978-1-0693414-4-0
Cover Design: Francis Williams
Published by: Quite Frank Educational Services
Printed in USA

"Amid the noise and haste, there is still peace.
Amid the chaos, there is still wisdom.
Amid the struggles, life remains beautiful.
The journey to serenity begins within."

~ Living Desiderata: Applying Its Poetic Wisdom
to Our Chaotic Times

.

"You have power over your mind - not outside
events. Realize this, and you will find strength."

~ Marcus Aurelius (*Meditations*)

"Happiness is not something ready-made. It comes
from your own actions."

~ Dalai Lama

To

Danielle Hebert

A Child of the Universe

No Less than the Trees and the Stars

Disclaimer

The content of this book, Living Desiderata: Applying Its Poetic Wisdom to Our Chaotic Times, is intended for informational and inspirational purposes only. While it explores themes of mindfulness, self-improvement, and philosophical reflection, it should not be considered a substitute for professional medical, psychological, financial, or legal advice.

The interpretations and insights provided in this book are based on the author's reflections on *Desiderata* by Max Ehrmann, as well as various philosophical, psychological, and spiritual concepts. Readers are encouraged to use their own judgment and discretion when applying any ideas or suggestions to their personal lives.

The author and publisher assume no responsibility for any outcomes resulting from the application of the material in this book. If you are experiencing significant emotional distress, mental health challenges, or other personal difficulties, it is recommended that you seek support from a qualified professional.

All references to historical figures, philosophies, and literary works are intended to provide context and do not imply endorsement or affiliation. The rights to *Desiderata* remain with the original author, Max Ehrmann, and this book serves as a reflective analysis rather than a reproduction of the original work.

By reading this book, you acknowledge and agree that your interpretation and application of the material are your personal responsibility.

Note to Readers

This book was created with the support of AI-assisted tools, which were used to help research, organize, and refine the material presented. While the insights, reflections, and interpretations are deeply rooted in the timeless wisdom of *Desiderata*, modern philosophical thought, and self-development principles, AI was used as an aid in structuring the content, generating ideas, and ensuring clarity in expression.

However, every concept, analysis, and interpretation remains grounded in human reflection, wisdom, and experience. The purpose of using AI in this process was not to replace creativity or personal insight but to enhance the efficiency of research and organization - allowing for a thoughtful and accessible exploration of *Desiderata*'s message.

As with any book, readers are encouraged to engage critically with the material, reflect on its meaning in their own lives, and apply it in ways that resonate with their personal journey.

Thank you for embarking on this exploration of *Desiderata* with an open heart and mind. May its wisdom continue to inspire you, now and always.

Living Desiderata: Applying Its Poetic Wisdom to Our Chaotic Times

Table of Contents

Introduction: The Enduring Power of Desiderata

In a world that often feels chaotic, divided, and uncertain, the wisdom of *Desiderata* offers a guiding light. Written by Max Ehrmann in 1927, this prose poem has endured through generations, offering solace, encouragement, and a quiet yet profound philosophy for life. Its words, simple yet powerful, remind us of the importance of peace, truth, humility, resilience, and hope - qualities that seem more necessary than ever in today's fast-paced and often overwhelming world.

Ehrmann's words transcend time and circumstance. Whether we find ourselves facing political turmoil, social unrest, personal struggles, or global crises, *Desiderata* reminds us that serenity is possible, that truth is worth speaking, and that our presence in the universe is meaningful. Its wisdom is not a rigid doctrine, but a gentle invitation to live with grace and purpose amid the uncertainty that life inevitably brings.

This book seeks to reflect on *Desiderata* not just as a poetic work, but as a living philosophy that we can apply to our daily lives. Each chapter will delve into one of its key messages, exploring how these timeless insights can help us navigate the modern world's challenges with wisdom and strength.

A Message for Our Times

We live in an age of unprecedented connectivity, yet isolation is more prevalent than ever. Social media has given everyone a voice, yet many struggle to be heard or understood. Information is abundant, yet wisdom often seems scarce. In this turbulent landscape, *Desiderata* offers a return to fundamental truths - reminding us to seek balance, practice kindness, and embrace the beauty of life even when it feels uncertain.

In recent years, mental health struggles have surged, political tensions have deepened, and the pace of life has become relentless. People find themselves constantly comparing their lives to curated images on screens, measuring their worth by external validation, and losing sight of their own intrinsic value. Ehrmann's advice - *do not compare yourself with others, for always there will be greater and lesser persons than yourself* - is a much-needed antidote to the anxiety and self-doubt that comparison breeds.

Similarly, his call to *nurture strength of spirit to shield you in sudden misfortune* speaks directly to our collective need for resilience in an era where uncertainty seems to be the only constant. Whether we are navigating personal losses, economic instability, or global crises, the ability to cultivate inner strength is essential.

The Beauty of Simplicity and Truth

What makes *Desiderata* so powerful is its simplicity. Unlike complex philosophical treatises or dense self-help books, it does not seek to overwhelm or intellectualize. Instead, it offers straightforward, heartfelt guidance - urging us to be gentle with ourselves and others, to move through life with dignity and patience, and to trust in the unfolding journey.

This book will explore each of these principles in depth, offering reflections on how they can be practically applied in our daily lives. Through personal stories, historical insights, and thoughtful analysis, we will uncover how *Desiderata* can help us find peace amid the noise, clarity in moments of confusion, and hope in times of despair.

A Journey of Reflection and Renewal

The goal of this book is not merely to analyze *Desiderata*, but to invite you into a personal reflection. As you read through each chapter, consider how its wisdom resonates with your own experiences. How can you embrace serenity amid chaos? Where in your life do you need to let go of comparison? What steps can you take to nurture strength of spirit?

In a world that often feels overwhelming, *Desiderata* remains a quiet, steadfast guide - a reminder that, despite the challenges we face, life is still beautiful, meaningful, and worth embracing.

So let us embark on this journey together, exploring the deep and timeless philosophy of *Desiderata* and discovering how its message can help us navigate the complexities of our modern world with grace, courage, and joy.

Chapter 1: Go Placidly Amid the Noise and Haste: Cultivating Inner Peace

The Call for Serenity in a Chaotic World

> "Go placidly amid the noise and haste, and remember what peace there may be in silence."

These opening words of *Desiderata* set the tone for the entire poem, offering a profound yet simple piece of wisdom: in the midst of life's chaos, cultivate peace. This is easier said than done, especially in a world that constantly demands our attention, fuels our anxieties, and thrives on urgency.

In today's world, noise surrounds us - both physically and mentally. From the moment we wake, we're flooded with notifications, headlines, and endless tasks. Life moves at a relentless pace, urging us forward without pause. In this environment, finding stillness is not just beneficial, it's essential. In such an environment, the idea of moving "placidly" may seem impossible, even naive. But in truth, it is one of the most essential skills we can cultivate.

The Power of Stillness

Inner peace does not mean withdrawing from life or ignoring its demands. It is not passivity or indifference. Rather, it is about developing a state of calm awareness - a centeredness that allows us to engage with the world without being consumed by its chaos.

One of the greatest lessons of *Desiderata* is that peace is not something we wait for; it is something we actively cultivate. The ability to "go placidly" is not a luxury reserved for monks or those living in solitude - it is a discipline that anyone can develop, regardless of their circumstances.

Consider historical figures who embodied this principle. Mahatma Gandhi, despite leading a movement against colonial rule, practiced inner stillness through meditation and simplicity. Nelson Mandela, even in the harshest conditions of imprisonment, maintained a sense of inner calm and purpose.

These examples remind us that external circumstances do not have to dictate our internal state.

The Modern-Day Struggle with Inner Peace

Our world presents unique challenges that make inner peace difficult to attain:

- **Information Overload:** We consume more information in a single day than people did in a lifetime just a few centuries ago. This constant stream of news, opinions, and stimuli creates a mental fog, making it difficult to think clearly or feel at ease.

- **The Culture of Busyness:** In modern society, being busy is often seen as a badge of honor. We equate productivity with worth, leaving little room for rest or reflection.

- **Social Media Noise:** We are constantly comparing our lives to the highlight reels of others, leading to anxiety, insecurity, and a sense of never being "enough."

- **Global Uncertainty:** Economic instability, political unrest, and environmental crises contribute to a collective sense of anxiety and urgency.

In light of these challenges, the call to "go placidly" is not just poetic advice - it is a radical and necessary act of self-preservation.

Practical Ways to Cultivate Serenity

How can we begin to move placidly amid the noise and haste? Here are a few practical steps:

1. Embrace the Power of Silence

In a world filled with constant chatter, silence is a rare and precious commodity. Taking intentional moments of silence - whether through meditation, a walk in nature, or simply sitting quietly - can help reset the mind and bring clarity.

- **Morning Stillness:** Start the day with a few minutes of quiet before checking your phone or engaging with the outside world.

- **Technology Breaks:** Designate specific times during the day to disconnect from screens and social media.

- **Mindful Listening:** Instead of rushing to respond in conversations, practice listening with full presence.

2. Slow Down

Speed is often mistaken for efficiency, but constant rushing creates stress and mistakes. Learning to slow down can actually enhance both productivity and peace.

- **Practice Mindful Walking:** Instead of rushing from place to place, walk with awareness, noticing your surroundings and breath.

- **Eat Without Distraction:** Avoid multitasking during meals; focus on the flavors, textures, and the experience of eating.

- **Single-Tasking Over Multitasking:** Focus on one task at a time rather than trying to juggle multiple things at once.

3. Create a Daily Ritual of Peace

Building peaceful habits into your daily routine can help cultivate long-term inner calm.

- **Journaling:** Writing down thoughts, worries, or reflections can bring clarity and emotional release.

- **Breathing Exercises:** Simple breathing techniques, like the 4-7-8 method (inhale for 4 seconds, hold for 7, exhale for 8), can quickly reduce stress.

- **Gratitude Practice:** Focusing on what you are grateful for shifts the mind from worry to contentment.

4. Redefine Success

Many of us chase achievements, believing that peace will come *after* success. But peace is not a destination; it is a way of traveling.

- **Let Go of Perfectionism:** Accept that mistakes and imperfections are part of life.

- **Detach from External Validation:** Recognize that self-worth is not determined by status, likes, or approval from others.

- **Prioritize Well-Being Over Productivity:** Sometimes, resting is the most productive thing you can do.

The Role of Perspective: Seeing Beyond the Noise

One of the greatest obstacles to serenity is our attachment to external circumstances. When we tie our sense of calm to things going our way, we set ourselves up for constant stress. Instead, cultivating peace requires a shift in perspective.

The Stoic philosophers, much like Ehrmann, taught that while we cannot always control what happens to us, we can control how we respond. Marcus Aurelius wrote, *"You have power over your mind - not outside events. Realize this, and you will find strength."*

Similarly, Buddhist teachings emphasize the idea of impermanence - that all things, including our troubles, are temporary. When we adopt this view, we stop clinging to the idea that peace is something that exists only when life is perfect. Instead, we learn to find peace even in imperfection.

Conclusion: The Path to Lasting Peace

The wisdom of *Desiderata* reminds us that peace is not about escaping the world but about learning to navigate it with grace. "Go placidly amid the noise and haste" is not an instruction to ignore reality but an invitation to cultivate a state of being that allows us to engage with life without being overwhelmed by it.

In times of personal stress, political turmoil, or societal upheaval, these words offer a steady anchor. They remind us that we do not have to be at the mercy of the chaos around us. We can choose to slow down, to breathe, to listen, and to embrace the stillness within.

And in that stillness, we find not only peace - but also strength.

Chapter 2: As Far as Possible Without Surrender – The Art of Compromise

The Delicate Balance Between Integrity and Harmony

"As far as possible, without surrender, be on good terms with all persons."

With these words, *Desiderata* offers a profound lesson in human relationships: strive for harmony, but not at the cost of your values. In a world increasingly defined by division, polarization, and ideological rigidity, this message is more relevant than ever. The art of compromise is an essential skill in maintaining both personal integrity and peaceful coexistence.

But what does it truly mean to be on good terms with all people *without surrender*? How do we balance kindness with self-respect, flexibility with authenticity? This chapter explores the fine line between compromise and concession, offering insights into how we can navigate relationships, conflicts, and disagreements with wisdom and grace.

The Necessity of Compromise in Human Relationships

Compromise is at the heart of all meaningful relationships - whether in family, friendship, workplace dynamics, or even global diplomacy. Without it, relationships deteriorate into power struggles, and societies descend into conflict. But compromise does not mean sacrificing one's core beliefs or becoming a people-pleaser.

In personal relationships, we often face moments where differing needs and expectations arise. A couple may have different views on finances, parenting, or career choices. Friends may disagree on values or political opinions. In the workplace, collaboration requires negotiation and a willingness to meet others halfway. In each of these cases, the ability to find common ground is essential for maintaining healthy and respectful connections.

Yet, compromise becomes harmful when it leads to self-betrayal. If we constantly suppress our feelings, ignore our needs, or sacrifice our values just to avoid conflict, we are not truly compromising - we are surrendering. The challenge is learning to distinguish between healthy flexibility and harmful submission.

Understanding Healthy vs. Unhealthy Compromise

To navigate compromise wisely, it's crucial to recognize the difference between constructive flexibility and destructive self-sacrifice.

Healthy Compromise:

✚ Involves mutual respect and consideration of both parties' needs.

✚ Maintains personal boundaries while remaining open to new perspectives.

✚ Strengthens relationships through shared understanding and cooperation.

✚ Allows for growth and adaptation without losing one's core values.

Unhealthy Compromise (Surrender):

X Involves giving in solely to avoid conflict, even at personal cost.

X Leads to resentment, frustration, and loss of self-respect.

X Creates an imbalance of power in relationships.

X Results in a diminished sense of identity and authenticity.

One of the greatest challenges of modern society is that people often see compromise as weakness. Many mistake stubbornness for strength and flexibility for fragility. However, true strength lies in knowing when to stand firm and when to yield.

The Dangers of Rigid Thinking

One of the main obstacles to healthy compromise is rigid thinking - the belief that any deviation from one's stance is a loss. We see this increasingly in politics, social movements, and personal interactions. The rise of cancel culture, ideological extremism, and a refusal to engage with differing viewpoints has led to greater division rather than understanding.

History offers countless examples of the power of compromise. The U.S. Constitution was formed through intense negotiations between opposing factions. Nelson Mandela, after decades of imprisonment, chose reconciliation over revenge, facilitating the peaceful transition of South Africa from apartheid to democracy. These examples remind us that progress often depends on a willingness to find middle ground.

However, there are also times when standing firm is necessary. Had figures like Mahatma Gandhi or Martin Luther King Jr. compromised their core principles, the world might look very different today. The wisdom of *Desiderata* lies in its nuance - it does not ask us to seek peace at any cost, but rather to pursue it as far as possible *without surrender.*

Practical Strategies for Balancing Compromise and Integrity

How do we apply this wisdom in our daily lives?

1. Know Your Core Values

Before entering any compromise, it's crucial to understand what is *non-negotiable* for you. These are the values and beliefs that define your character and moral compass.

- Ask yourself: What are my fundamental principles?
- Where am I willing to be flexible, and where must I stand firm?
- Will this compromise strengthen or diminish my sense of self?

For example, if honesty is a core value, agreeing to lie for someone - even in a small matter - would be a harmful compromise. However, if the issue is choosing a restaurant for dinner, yielding to someone else's preference may be a healthy and minor concession.

2. Listen with Openness, Not Just to Respond

In conflicts, most people listen with the intent to reply, not to understand. True compromise requires *empathetic listening* - seeking to genuinely understand the other person's perspective.

- Pause before responding in disagreements.

- Ask clarifying questions: "Can you help me understand why this is important to you?"

- Acknowledge the other person's viewpoint, even if you don't agree.

When people feel heard, they are more likely to reciprocate and seek a middle ground.

3. Express Your Needs Clearly and Calmly

Many people struggle with compromise because they either:

1. **Suppress their needs**, leading to silent resentment.

2. **Express their needs aggressively**, leading to conflict.

Instead, assertiveness - the ability to communicate clearly and respectfully - is key.

- Instead of saying: *"You never listen to me!"*
  Consider: *"I feel unheard when my concerns are dismissed. Can we find a way to address this together?"*

- Instead of saying: *"I can't believe you think that way!"*
  Consider: *"I see this differently, but I'd like to understand your perspective."*

Clear, calm communication fosters mutual understanding without hostility.

4. Set Boundaries with Grace

Boundaries are not walls - they are guidelines for healthy interaction. Saying "no" does not make you unkind; it makes you self-respecting.

- Practice saying "no" without guilt: *"I appreciate your perspective, but I'm not comfortable with that decision."*

- Use boundary-setting as a tool for preserving relationships rather than breaking them: *"I value our friendship, but I need to take some space to process this disagreement."*

5. Accept That You Can't Please Everyone

One of the biggest traps in compromise is the fear of disappointing others. But trying to keep everyone happy often leads to personal exhaustion.

- Remind yourself: **Not everyone has to agree with you, and that's okay.**

- Focus on maintaining self-respect rather than universal approval.

- Accept that some relationships may change when you set boundaries - and that's a natural part of growth.

Conclusion: Finding Strength in Balance

The wisdom of *Desiderata* teaches us that peace in relationships is worth striving for - but not at the expense of our integrity. The goal is not to avoid conflict at all costs, nor is it to win every argument. Instead, it is to navigate human interactions with grace, wisdom, and a clear understanding of our own worth.

Compromise is an art. It requires patience, self-awareness, and a willingness to see beyond our own perspectives. When done wisely, it does not weaken us - it strengthens both our relationships and our sense of self.

So as you move through life's inevitable conflicts, remember: seek harmony, but never at the cost of surrendering who you are.

Chapter 3: Speak Your Truth Quietly and Clearly – The Strength of Gentle Honesty

The Power of Truth in a World of Noise

"Speak your truth quietly and clearly; and listen to others, even the dull and the ignorant; they too have their story."

This line from *Desiderata* carries a profound lesson in communication. It reminds us that truth, when spoken with wisdom and humility, has far greater power than the loudest voice in the room. It also challenges us to listen - to recognize that every person, no matter how unremarkable or different from us, has a story worth hearing.

We live in an age of constant opinions. Social media platforms encourage rapid responses, public debates, and even outrage culture. The loudest voices often get the most attention, while those who speak with quiet wisdom are overlooked. Many people either shy away from speaking their truth for fear of backlash or, conversely, insist on making their point aggressively, alienating those around them.

But *Desiderata* offers a different approach - one rooted in confidence, clarity, and respect. In this chapter, we will explore what it means to speak your truth quietly and clearly, why gentle honesty is more powerful than aggression, and how deep listening transforms relationships and communities.

The Essence of Speaking Your Truth

Speaking your truth does not mean forcing your beliefs on others or engaging in endless arguments. Instead, it means:

+ Expressing your thoughts, feelings, and beliefs with confidence but without arrogance.

+ Communicating in a way that fosters understanding rather than division.

+ Honoring your values while respecting the perspectives of others.

At its core, this principle is about authenticity. When you speak your truth, you live in alignment with your values, rather than suppressing your voice to please others or inflating your presence to overpower them.

Consider some of history's most respected leaders - Mahatma Gandhi, the Dalai Lama, Mother Teresa. They did not need to shout to be heard. Their quiet strength and unwavering truth made them powerful beyond measure. Their words resonated not because they were the loudest, but because they were spoken with clarity, sincerity, and purpose.

The modern world, however, encourages a different model. Loudness is often mistaken for leadership. Controversy is rewarded with attention. Fear of disagreement keeps many people silent. But true strength lies in the ability to speak with calm conviction, not in the volume of one's voice.

Why Gentleness is More Powerful Than Aggression

Many assume that being heard requires forcefulness—that raising one's voice ensures attention. Yet history and psychology reveal a different truth: quiet conviction often carries the most weight.

1. **Aggression Creates Resistance**

   o When someone feels attacked, they become defensive rather than receptive.

   o Forceful arguments may win debates, but they rarely change hearts.

2. **Gentle Honesty Encourages Openness**

   o When people feel safe in a conversation, they are more likely to listen and reflect.

   o A calm tone disarms hostility and invites meaningful dialogue.

3. **Quiet Strength Commands Respect**

   o Those who speak with measured confidence are often taken more seriously than those who yell.

   o A soft but firm voice can hold a room better than one filled with anger or arrogance.

A simple example: Imagine two people presenting their viewpoints. One shouts, interrupts, and refuses to consider other perspectives. The other speaks steadily, listens, and responds with clarity and kindness. Who is more likely to earn respect and create change?

Even in personal relationships, a quiet but firm voice carries more influence than emotional outbursts. Consider a workplace setting where a leader remains calm under pressure. Their quiet assurance reassures the team far more than a boss who yells or panics.

How to Speak Your Truth Quietly and Clearly

To practice this principle in daily life, consider the following strategies:

1. Speak With Confidence, Not Apology

Many people dilute their own voices with hesitation, disclaimers, or self-doubt. Pay attention to how you express yourself.

X Instead of: *"This may not be important, but I just wanted to say..."*

✚ Consider: *"I believe this is important because..."*

X Instead of: *"I could be wrong, but..."*

✚ Consider: *"Based on my understanding, I see it this way."*

Confidence does not mean arrogance. It simply means you trust your perspective while remaining open to new insights.

2. Use a Calm and Measured Tone

The way we say something is just as important as what we say. A calm, steady voice is more persuasive than an aggressive one.

- Take deep breaths before responding in difficult conversations.

- Lower your voice slightly when making an important point - this often draws people in.

- Avoid rushing; allow pauses to let your words sink in.

3. Choose Your Words Wisely

Not all truths need to be spoken, and not all battles need to be fought.

- Before speaking, ask: *Is this necessary? Is it helpful? Is it kind?*

- When offering criticism, frame it constructively: *"I think this could be improved by..."* instead of *"This is completely wrong."*

- Avoid absolutes like *"You always..."* or *"You never..."* which tend to escalate conflict.

4. Stay True to Your Values, Even Under Pressure

In moments of conflict, it can be tempting to either back down or lash out. The challenge is to stand firm *without hostility*.

- If someone challenges your beliefs, respond with steady clarity: *"I see this differently, and here's why."*

- If pressured to conform, gently but firmly decline: *"That's not something I'm comfortable with."*

Staying true to your values does not mean shutting down dialogue - it means engaging with integrity.

Conclusion: The Strength of Gentle Honesty

The wisdom of *Desiderata* teaches us that truth is not about volume, but clarity. It is not about dominance, but integrity. To speak our truth quietly and clearly is to embrace a rare kind of strength - one that does not seek to overpower, but to enlighten.

At the same time, we must also listen. Even those we might dismiss have stories worth hearing. By balancing honest expression with open-hearted listening, we cultivate not only wisdom but also genuine connection with the world around us.

In an age of noise, may we choose clarity. In a time of division, may we choose understanding. And in a world that rewards the loudest voices, may we remember the quiet power of truth.

Chapter 4: Listen to Others, Even the Dull and the Ignorant – Finding Wisdom in All Voices

The Value of Listening in a Divided World

"Listen to others, even the dull and the ignorant; they too have their story."

These words from *Desiderata* offer a profound challenge. They ask us to go beyond our natural biases, to listen not just to those we admire or agree with, but also to those we might dismiss.

In today's world, listening has become a lost art. Conversations often turn into debates, where people listen only to respond, not to understand. Social media amplifies this divide, creating echo chambers where opposing views are ridiculed rather than engaged with. The result? A society where people speak at each other rather than with each other.

Yet, the ability to listen deeply - to hear beyond words, to see the humanity in others - is one of the most powerful skills we can cultivate. It fosters understanding, defuses conflict, and opens the door to unexpected wisdom.

In this chapter, we will explore why true listening is rare, how dismissing others leads to missed opportunities for growth, and how we can practice deep and intentional listening in our daily lives.

The Ego's Obstacle: Why We Struggle to Listen

Most people believe they are good listeners. But in reality, listening is difficult because it requires setting aside our own judgments, opinions, and ego.

Why We Dismiss Others

1. **We Judge Intelligence Based on Presentation**

    o We are quick to dismiss people based on how they speak, their level of education, or their vocabulary.

    o A person who struggles to articulate their thoughts is often overlooked, even if they have deep wisdom.

2. **We Assume We Already Know**

    o When someone speaks, we often think, *"I've heard this before,"* and mentally check out.

    o This prevents us from recognizing fresh perspectives or deeper insights hidden in familiar words.

3. **We Are Preoccupied with Our Own Thoughts**

    o Instead of truly listening, we often spend conversations planning our response.

    o We prioritize our next argument over fully understanding the other person's point.

4. **We Fear Being Challenged**

    o Listening to different perspectives requires humility. It forces us to consider the possibility that we may be wrong or that our worldview is incomplete.

Because of these tendencies, many voices go unheard - especially those we consider "dull and ignorant." But *Desiderata* reminds us that everyone has a story. And often, wisdom comes from the most unexpected places.

The Hidden Wisdom in Every Person

Throughout history, some of the greatest insights have come from ordinary, overlooked individuals.

- **Socrates**, one of the most brilliant philosophers of all time, claimed to know nothing and spent his life listening and questioning. His wisdom came not from asserting ideas but from drawing them out of others.

- **Abraham Lincoln**, during the American Civil War, made it a point to meet with everyday citizens - farmers, soldiers, and laborers - because he believed wisdom was not limited to the educated elite.

- **Albert Einstein**, despite his genius, often credited simple conversations with ordinary people for helping him clarify his theories.

Wisdom is not confined to scholars, leaders, or intellectuals. It can come from a child's innocent question, a stranger's passing remark, or a conversation with someone whose life experience is vastly different from our own.

Consider the janitor who has observed human behavior for decades, the elderly woman at the bus stop who has lived through history, or the cashier who sees a hundred different personalities a day. Each of these individuals carries insights that we may never have considered - if only we take the time to listen.

Practical Steps to Becoming a Better Listener

How do we cultivate the ability to listen deeply and without judgment?

1. Listen Without Preparing Your Response

One of the biggest barriers to true listening is our tendency to plan our next words while the other person is speaking.

- Practice pausing before responding.

- Repeat back what the other person has said in your own words to ensure you understood them correctly.

- Ask yourself: *Am I truly listening, or just waiting for my turn to speak?*

2. Approach Every Conversation with Curiosity

Instead of dismissing people, approach each interaction as an opportunity to learn something new.

- Try asking, *"What can I learn from this person?"*

- Even if you disagree, ask, *"What life experiences might have led them to this belief?"*

When we listen with curiosity rather than judgment, we often find unexpected insights.

3. Pay Attention to Nonverbal Communication

Listening is not just about words - it's about observing body language, tone, and emotions.

- Notice the expressions, pauses, and gestures of the speaker.

- Sometimes, what is left unsaid reveals more than the words themselves.

4. Resist the Urge to Correct or Debate

We often listen with the intent to argue or correct, especially when we disagree. But true listening means allowing space for other perspectives to exist.

- Instead of saying, *"That's wrong,"* try: *"That's interesting. Can you tell me more?"*

- Instead of shutting down the conversation, ask open-ended questions that encourage deeper discussion.

5. Give People the Benefit of the Doubt

Instead of labeling someone as ignorant or dull, consider that they may have knowledge or experiences that you lack.

- Assume that every person you meet knows something that you don't.

- Practice humility in conversation - acknowledge that your perspective is limited.

The Transformational Power of Listening

When we truly listen, something incredible happens:

1. **We Build Deeper Connections**

   o People feel valued when they are heard.

   o Meaningful conversations strengthen relationships, whether with family, friends, or colleagues.

2. **We Reduce Conflict**

   o Many arguments stem from misunderstandings.

   o When people feel heard, they are less defensive and more open to compromise.

3. **We Expand Our Perspective**

    o   Listening to different viewpoints makes us wiser and more adaptable.

    o   We become more empathetic, understanding, and open-minded.

4. **We Become More Respected**

    o   Those who listen deeply are often the most respected people in any group.

    o   Being known as a good listener makes others trust and seek out your company.

Conclusion: Hearing the Voices That Matter

"Listen to others, even the dull and the ignorant; they too have their story."

This is not just a call for politeness - it is a call for wisdom. When we dismiss others, we limit our own understanding. When we listen deeply, we open ourselves to unexpected insights, deeper relationships, and a richer perspective on life.

In a world filled with noise, may we choose to be listeners. In a society obsessed with talking, may we find strength in silence. And in a time when people struggle to be heard, may we be the ones who truly listen.

Because wisdom does not only belong to the loudest voices. Sometimes, it is found in the quietest ones.

Chapter 5: Avoid Loud and Aggressive Persons – Protecting Your Mental Space

The Impact of Toxic Energy on Peace of Mind

"Avoid loud and aggressive persons; they are vexatious to the spirit."

These words from *Desiderata* serve as both a warning and a piece of timeless wisdom. They remind us that not all company is beneficial and that the energy we surround ourselves with affects our well-being.

In today's world, where aggression is often mistaken for confidence and loudness for leadership, it can be difficult to avoid those who drain our energy. Whether in our personal relationships, workplaces, or even the digital world, we frequently encounter people who thrive on conflict, manipulation, or negativity. While it is not always possible to physically remove ourselves from such individuals, we can learn how to protect our inner peace.

This chapter will explore the different types of loud and aggressive people, how their presence can affect our mental and emotional health, and strategies for setting healthy boundaries while maintaining our serenity.

Recognizing Loud and Aggressive Personalities

Not all "loud" people are problematic - some are simply energetic, passionate, or extroverted. The problem arises when loudness is accompanied by aggression, negativity, or a disregard for others' peace of mind. These individuals can manifest in different ways:

1. The Constant Critic

- Always finds flaws in everything and everyone.

- Rarely offers constructive feedback - just relentless negativity.

- Leaves you feeling small, inadequate, or drained.

2. The Perpetual Arguer

- Seeks conflict, whether online or in person.

- Never listens, only wants to "win" conversations.

- Often uses anger or intimidation to dominate discussions.

3. The Drama Magnet

- Thrives on creating or exaggerating conflicts.

- Drains emotional energy by constantly seeking attention.

- Often makes problems seem bigger than they are.

4. The Overbearing Authority

- Believes their way is the only way.

- Uses loudness to control or manipulate situations.

- Leaves little room for others to express their opinions.

5. The Chronic Complainer

- Always finds something to be unhappy about.

- Drains positivity from conversations.

- Never seeks solutions - only validation for their complaints.

Recognizing these behaviors is the first step toward protecting your peace. Some of these individuals may not even be aware of the impact they have on others. However, our responsibility is not to fix them, but to protect our mental and emotional well-being.

The Cost of Exposure to Negative Energy

Being around loud and aggressive people for extended periods can have a profound effect on our well-being. Even if we believe we are unaffected, their energy can seep into our subconscious, shaping our mood and outlook.

1. Increased Stress and Anxiety

- Aggressive energy triggers the body's fight-or-flight response, leading to prolonged stress.

- Constant negativity can create anxiety, making it harder to relax and focus.

2. Emotional Drain and Burnout

- Interacting with aggressive people takes a toll on emotional energy.

- Over time, we may feel exhausted, unmotivated, or even resentful.

3. Erosion of Self-Worth

- Constant criticism or loud dominance can make us doubt our own opinions and value.

- A toxic environment can lead to self-censorship or fear of speaking up.

4. Distorted Perception of Reality

- When surrounded by negativity, we may start to believe the world is as hopeless as these individuals describe.

- This can lead to cynicism, pessimism, and a loss of faith in others.

By recognizing these effects, we can begin to take steps to protect our peace and mental space.

How to Protect Your Inner Peace

Avoiding loud and aggressive people doesn't necessarily mean cutting off everyone who frustrates us. It means developing strategies to maintain our serenity, even in challenging environments.

1. Set Firm Boundaries

You are not obligated to absorb anyone else's negativity. Boundaries help you protect your emotional energy without engaging in unnecessary conflict.

- **Limit exposure** – If possible, spend less time with aggressive individuals.

- **Keep interactions short and neutral** – Avoid deep conversations that invite conflict.

- **Politely disengage** – Say, *"I'd rather not discuss this topic,"* and change the subject.

2. Stay Calm in the Face of Aggression

Aggressive people often feed off reactions. By refusing to engage emotionally, you deny them power over your peace.

- **Remain neutral** – Respond with calmness rather than matching their energy.

- **Use short responses** – Sometimes, a simple *"I see your point"* or *"That's interesting"* is enough to disengage.

- **Take deep breaths** – Ground yourself in the present moment to avoid reacting impulsively.

3. Choose Your Battles Wisely

Not every argument needs your participation. Sometimes, the best response is no response.

- **Ask yourself** – *Will this conversation lead to growth or just frustration?*

- **Walk away if necessary** – You are not obligated to stay in negative energy.

4. Create an Inner Sanctuary

If you must be around aggressive people (workplace, family, etc.), it's important to build a mental refuge.

- **Develop mindfulness practices** – Meditation, deep breathing, or nature walks help reset your mind.

- **Surround yourself with positive influences** – Counteract negativity by spending time with uplifting people.

- **Protect your digital space** – Limit exposure to online negativity by curating your social media feed.

5. Practice the Art of Detachment

Emotional detachment does not mean indifference - it means choosing not to be emotionally manipulated.

- **See beyond their words** – Recognize that aggression is often a symptom of personal insecurity or pain.

- **Let go of the need to "fix" them** – You cannot change people, only your response to them.

- **Visualize a protective barrier** – Imagine yourself surrounded by an invisible shield that keeps negativity out.

When to Walk Away Completely

In some cases, avoidance is not just preferable - it is necessary. If someone consistently drains your energy, disrespects your boundaries, or causes you emotional distress, it may be time to distance yourself completely.

- **Toxic relationships** – If a friend, family member, or partner constantly brings negativity into your life without accountability, consider stepping away.

- **Hostile work environments** – If a job is affecting your mental health due to aggressive coworkers or a toxic boss, exploring other opportunities may be beneficial.

- **Social media detox** – If online spaces create more frustration than insight, take breaks or curate your digital interactions.

Walking away does not mean weakness - it means prioritizing your well-being.

Conclusion: Choosing Peace Over Chaos

"Avoid loud and aggressive persons; they are vexatious to the spirit."

This advice from *Desiderata* is more than just a reminder to steer clear of negativity - it is an invitation to intentionally cultivate peace. Loud and aggressive people exist everywhere, but we have the power to control how we engage with them.

By setting boundaries, choosing calm responses, and maintaining our inner sanctuary, we protect our peace without being consumed by external noise. The world is already filled with enough conflict - our greatest act of strength may be choosing not to add to it.

In the end, protecting our mental space is not about avoiding all difficult people, but about learning to navigate them with wisdom, grace, and unshakable serenity.

Chapter 6: Enjoy Your Achievements as Well as Your Plans – The Balance of Past and Future

The Art of Living in the Present

"Enjoy your achievements as well as your plans."

With this simple yet profound line, *Desiderata* reminds us of a fundamental truth: life is not just about striving - it is also about appreciating. We live in a world that glorifies ambition, urging us to constantly push forward, set new goals, and reach for the next milestone. While there is great value in planning and striving, there is also a danger: we can become so fixated on what's next that we forget to enjoy what we have already accomplished.

This chapter explores the delicate balance between ambition and contentment, why celebrating our achievements is just as important as setting new goals, and how we can live in the present while still embracing the future.

The Problem with Always Looking Ahead

Society pushes us to constantly achieve—to do more, be more, and plan ahead. From childhood, we learn to chase milestones: study hard, earn good grades, secure a prestigious job. But in this pursuit, we risk overlooking the present. We are conditioned to think ahead:

- Study hard to get good grades.
- Get good grades to get into a good university.
- Get into a good university to get a good job.
- Get a good job to afford a house, start a family, and secure retirement.

While long-term planning is important, this mindset can create a dangerous cycle - one in which we are always chasing the next thing and never fully appreciating where we are.

Signs You Might Be Living Too Much in the Future

+ You achieve something significant but quickly move on to the next goal without pausing to celebrate.

+ You feel restless or dissatisfied, no matter how much you accomplish.

+ You equate success with *what's next* rather than *what's now*.

+ You struggle to enjoy downtime because you feel like you *should* be working toward something.

Ambition is not the problem - the problem is when ambition prevents us from feeling joy in the present moment.

Why Celebrating Your Achievements Matters

When we acknowledge and celebrate what we have already accomplished, we experience several benefits:

1. It Reinforces Confidence and Motivation

Every achievement - big or small - deserves recognition. If we never stop to appreciate our progress, we risk feeling like we are never *enough*. Taking time to acknowledge success builds confidence and reminds us that we are capable.

- **Reflect on this:** Keep a *Victory Journal* where you write down even small accomplishments. Reading back through your wins can boost motivation when you feel stuck.

2. It Prevents Burnout

Pushing forward relentlessly without acknowledging past efforts leads to exhaustion. Resting, reflecting, and celebrating are crucial parts of sustainable success.

- **Reflect on this:** After completing a major task, give yourself a moment to pause - whether that's taking a break, treating yourself, or simply reflecting on what you've done.

3. It Cultivates Gratitude and Fulfillment

True fulfillment comes not from *just* reaching new goals, but from appreciating the journey. Recognizing what you have already achieved fosters a sense of gratitude and contentment.

- **Reflect on this:** Before setting a new goal, reflect on past successes and express gratitude for how far you've come.

The Power of Planning for the Future

While appreciating the present is essential, so is looking ahead. Dreams and goals give us direction and purpose.

Why Having a Vision Matters

- ✚ It gives life meaning and a sense of purpose.
- ✚ It helps us stay motivated and resilient in difficult times.
- ✚ It prevents stagnation and encourages personal growth.

Without plans, life can feel aimless. But, just as we must avoid obsessing over the future, we must also avoid fearing it.

Striking the Balance: Enjoying Achievements While Embracing the Future

So how do we enjoy our achievements *and* our plans? The key is learning how to live in both worlds simultaneously - acknowledging past success while remaining excited for what's ahead.

1. Reflect on Your Journey Without Getting Stuck in It

Sometimes, people get so attached to past achievements that they stop growing. They dwell on *former* successes rather than seeking new challenges.

- **Healthy reflection:** *"I'm proud of what I've done, and I'm excited for what's next."*

- **Unhealthy reflection:** *"I peaked in the past. Nothing will ever be as good again."*

Reflect on this: Write a letter to your past self, thanking them for their efforts and acknowledging how they contributed to where you are today.

2. Find Joy in the Process, Not Just the Outcome

The journey is just as important as the destination. If we only celebrate *after* reaching a goal, we miss countless moments of joy along the way.

- Instead of thinking, *"I'll be happy when I reach this milestone,"* try, *"I am grateful for this step in the process."*

- Learn to find fulfillment in the daily work, not just in the final result.

Reflect on this: After working on something meaningful, take a moment to appreciate the effort, even if the final goal is still far away.

3. Set Intentional Goals That Align with Your Values

Not all goals are created equal. Some are driven by external pressures, while others come from true personal desires.Before setting a new goal, ask yourself:

✚ *Is this something I truly want, or am I doing it because I think I should?*

✚ *Will this bring me fulfillment, or is it just another item on a checklist?*

✚ *Does this align with my deeper values and aspirations?*

Goals should serve your personal growth and happiness, not just your productivity.

4. Celebrate Small Wins Along the Way

People often wait until they reach a major milestone to celebrate. But every small step matters.

- Finished a difficult project? Celebrate.

- Learned something new? Celebrate.

- Took a step out of your comfort zone? Celebrate.

Reflect on this: Set up a reward system for yourself. For every small goal completed, allow yourself a moment of joy - whether it's a break, a treat, or simply a moment of gratitude.

Living Fully in Both the Present and the Future

Enjoying your achievements and making plans for the future are not opposing ideas - they are complementary. True happiness comes from the ability to embrace both.

- **Enjoy your achievements:** Reflect on how far you've come, acknowledge your efforts, and take pride in your progress.

- **Embrace your plans:** Continue dreaming, setting new goals, and striving toward growth.

- **Live in the moment:** Appreciate *now* rather than always waiting for the "next big thing."

The key to a fulfilling life is finding the balance between *appreciation* and *aspiration*.

Conclusion: The Wisdom of Enough

"Enjoy your achievements as well as your plans."

These words from *Desiderata* invite us to step off the endless treadmill of achievement and pause, even if just for a moment, to appreciate what we have already done.

They remind us that life is not only about forward motion but also about reflection and gratitude. They teach us that while it is good to dream, it is also essential to *live* - to find joy in the process, to celebrate small victories, and to recognize that happiness is not *just* in the destination, but in the journey itself.

So, take a breath. Look around. Appreciate where you are *now*. The future will come, and when it does, it will be built upon the foundation of all that you have already achieved.

Chapter 7: Exercise Caution in Your Business Affairs – The Ethics of Success

Navigating Success with Integrity

"Exercise caution in your business affairs; for the world is full of trickery."

These words from *Desiderata* serve as a timeless warning: while ambition and financial success are valuable, they must be pursued with wisdom, integrity, and caution. In a world where business dealings often prioritize profit over ethics, where deception can be disguised as opportunity, and where competition sometimes overrides fairness, maintaining one's moral compass is both a challenge and a necessity.

The pursuit of success - whether in business, career, or financial stability - requires discernment. There will always be opportunities that seem too good to be true, individuals who exploit trust for personal gain, and situations that test one's values. However, exercising caution does not mean becoming cynical or distrusting - it means being mindful, informed, and principled in how we navigate our professional and financial lives.

This chapter explores the importance of ethical success, how to recognize and avoid deception, and the strategies for achieving both prosperity and integrity in business and career.

The World of Trickery: Recognizing Deception in Business

Trickery in business is not new. History is filled with stories of fraud, unethical leadership, and manipulative business practices. The challenge today is that trickery has evolved - it is often subtle, wrapped in persuasive marketing, fine print, and misleading promises.

Common Forms of Trickery in Business Affairs

1. Get-Rich-Quick Schemes

- Promises of unrealistic financial returns with minimal effort.

- Pyramid schemes, Ponzi schemes, and fraudulent investment opportunities.

- "Exclusive insider" opportunities that require upfront payment.

✛ Red flag: If something sounds too good to be true, it probably is.

2. Dishonest Business Practices

- Companies that exploit workers, deceive customers, or hide crucial information.

- Misleading contracts with hidden fees or obligations.

- Ethical "gray areas" where profits are prioritized over fairness.

✛ Red flag: If a deal requires secrecy, aggressive persuasion, or manipulation, it may lack integrity.

3. Workplace Deception

- False promises of career growth without real opportunity.

- Toxic leadership that manipulates employees with fear or false incentives.

- Corporate environments where ethics are sacrificed for short-term gains.

✛ Red flag: If a workplace culture relies on dishonesty or exploitation, it may not align with long-term success.

By understanding these forms of deception, we can take proactive steps to avoid falling into their traps.

The Cost of Unethical Success

Some people believe that success requires bending the rules or prioritizing profits over principles. However, history and experience show that unethical success often comes with a heavy price.

1. Loss of Reputation and Trust

- Businesses and individuals who deceive others eventually lose credibility.
- Once trust is broken, rebuilding it is difficult - sometimes impossible.
- A good name is more valuable than short-term financial gain.

2. Internal Conflict and Stress

- Living with dishonesty creates psychological tension.
- Many who achieve success unethically struggle with guilt, anxiety, and regret.
- True success includes peace of mind, not just financial wealth.

3. Legal and Financial Consequences

- Many who engage in unethical business practices eventually face legal trouble.
- Scandals, lawsuits, and fines can destroy what was built dishonestly.
- Sustainable success is built on integrity, not deception.

The best business affairs are those conducted with caution, transparency, and a commitment to fairness.

Exercising Caution: Principles for Ethical and Smart Business Affairs

How do we navigate the business world with wisdom while still achieving success? The key is to practice discernment and ethical decision-making.

1. Do Your Due Diligence

- Research before committing to any business venture, job, or investment.
- Verify the credibility of partners, employers, and opportunities.
- Read contracts carefully - never sign something you don't fully understand.

+ Rule of Thumb: *If you don't understand it, don't invest in it.*

2. Prioritize Long-Term Integrity Over Short-Term Gains

- Ethical businesses and careers may take longer to build, but they last longer.
- Avoid shortcuts that require compromising values.
- Think beyond immediate profits - consider the legacy you are building.

+ Ask Yourself: *Would I be proud of this decision in 10 years?*

3. Surround Yourself with Honest and Ethical People

- Choose business partners, colleagues, and mentors who value integrity.
- Avoid those who pressure you into unethical decisions.
- A strong, honest network leads to more sustainable opportunities.

+ Keep in mind: *Your reputation is shaped by the company you keep.*

4. Trust Your Instincts

- If something feels off, investigate further or walk away.

- Don't let pressure, greed, or desperation push you into a bad decision.

- Your inner sense of right and wrong is one of your greatest tools.

✚ **Wisdom Tip:** *Listen to intuition - it often detects problems before logic does.*

5. Give More Than You Take

- Ethical success is about contributing value, not just extracting wealth.

- Build businesses and careers that uplift others, not just yourself.

- The most successful and respected people are those who serve and create value.

✚ **Ask Yourself:** *Am I leaving people and situations better than I found them?*

Examples of Ethical Success

Many successful individuals and companies have thrived while maintaining their integrity:

- **Warren Buffett** – Known for his ethical investing principles, transparency, and long-term vision.

- **Patagonia (clothing brand)** – Built a profitable business while prioritizing environmental sustainability and fair labor.

- **Oprah Winfrey** – Used her platform not just for personal success, but to uplift and inspire others.

These examples prove that success and ethics are not mutually exclusive - they can, and should, go hand in hand.

Conclusion: Success With Caution and Integrity

"Exercise caution in your business affairs; for the world is full of trickery."

This line from *Desiderata* is a reminder that while ambition is good, wisdom is necessary. In a world where deception exists, we must navigate with caution - not fear, but careful awareness.

True success is not just about financial gain - it is about building something meaningful, sustainable, and honest. It is about protecting our integrity, maintaining trust, and ensuring that our professional endeavors align with our values.

As you move forward in your career, business, and financial life, remember:

- **Be wise, not fearful.**
- **Be discerning, not cynical.**
- **Be ambitious, but never at the cost of your integrity.**

In the end, the richest life is not the one filled with the most money, but the one filled with the most meaning.

Chapter 8: Be Yourself – The Liberation of Authenticity

The Freedom in Being Your True Self

"Be yourself."

These two simple words from *Desiderata* carry an immense depth of wisdom. In a world where social pressure, expectations, and comparisons constantly shape our behavior, staying true to oneself can feel like a radical act. From childhood, we are taught to fit in, to meet societal standards, and to seek validation from others. Yet, true happiness and inner peace come not from conforming but from embracing who we truly are.

This chapter explores the importance of authenticity, the challenges that prevent people from being themselves, and practical steps to live a life that is fully and unapologetically your own.

The Struggle Against Conformity

From an early age, we are conditioned to seek approval. Parents, teachers, peers, and society at large shape our beliefs about what is "acceptable." While some of these influences are positive, many of them push us toward conformity at the expense of our true selves.

How We Lose Ourselves in the Process

1. **Seeking External Validation**

   o Many people base their self-worth on how others perceive them.

   o Likes on social media, compliments, and external praise become measures of self-esteem.

2. **Fear of Judgment**

   o The fear of being criticized or rejected prevents people from expressing their true thoughts and desires.

   o Instead of standing out, many choose to blend in, even at the cost of their happiness.

3. **Playing Roles to Please Others**

   o Many people wear masks - adapting their personalities to fit different situations.

   o They suppress their true thoughts to avoid conflict or to be liked.

4. **Comparing Ourselves to Others**

   o Social media distorts reality, encouraging endless comparisons. The pressure to measure up often overshadows self-acceptance, leading people to chase someone else's path rather than embracing their own."

   o Instead of embracing their unique journey, many people try to replicate someone else's path.

The result? Many people go through life feeling disconnected from themselves, living according to expectations rather than desires.

The Power of Authenticity

Being yourself is not just about self-expression - it is about living with integrity, confidence, and freedom.

Why Authenticity Matters

✚ It Leads to True Happiness

- When you live authentically, you align with your values and passions, leading to genuine fulfillment.

✚ It Attracts the Right People

- The more you express your true self, the more you attract people who appreciate you for who you really are.

✚ It Reduces Stress

- Pretending to be someone else is exhausting. Living authentically removes the pressure of maintaining a false identity.

✚ It Builds Confidence

- The more comfortable you become with who you are, the less you need validation from others.

✚ It Inspires Others

- People who are unapologetically themselves give others permission to do the same.

In a world where many people are afraid to be different, authenticity is a superpower.

Overcoming the Fear of Being Yourself

Living authentically requires courage. It means being willing to stand apart, to embrace your uniqueness, and to let go of the need for constant approval.

1. Stop Seeking Approval from Everyone

- Not everyone will like you, and that's okay.

- The goal is not to please everyone, but to be at peace with yourself.

+ Reflect on this: The next time you feel the need to seek approval, ask yourself, *"Am I doing this because I truly want to, or because I want others to approve of me?"*

2. Identify Your Core Values

- Authenticity means living according to *your* values, not someone else's.

- Take time to reflect on what truly matters to you.

+ Reflect on this: Write down your top 5 values and use them as a guide for decision-making.

3. Accept Your Imperfections

- Chasing perfection is chasing a mirage..

- Embracing your flaws makes you more real and relatable.

+ Reflect on this: Instead of criticizing yourself for a flaw, reframe it as part of your uniqueness.

4. Let Go of Comparison

- Your journey is unique - comparing yourself to others only leads to insecurity.

- Focus on progress, not perfection.

+ Reflect on this: The next time you compare yourself to someone else, shift your focus to something you appreciate about yourself.

5. Express Yourself Without Fear

- Whether through your words, style, art, or actions - find ways to express your true self.

- The world needs your uniqueness, not your imitation of someone else.

+ Reflect on this: Start small - say what you really think in a conversation, wear what makes you feel good, or pursue a hobby that excites you.

Living Authentically in a World That Tries to Change You

Society often rewards conformity and punishes those who stand out. But those who leave the greatest impact are those who dare to be themselves.

Famous Examples of Authenticity

- **Albert Einstein** – He embraced his unconventional way of thinking, leading to groundbreaking discoveries.

- **Frida Kahlo** – She expressed her true self through art, refusing to conform to traditional beauty standards.

- **Steve Jobs** – His refusal to follow conventional business norms led to the creation of Apple.

These individuals changed the world *because* they were different, not in spite of it.

Conclusion: The Joy of Being Yourself

"Be yourself."

This is more than advice - it is a philosophy for living a life that is true, fulfilling, and meaningful. When you embrace who you are, you experience a sense of freedom that no external validation can provide.

You do not need to be like anyone else. You do not need to fit into society's mold. You are enough as you are.

So be yourself. Unapologetically. Boldly. Authentically.

The world doesn't need another copy. It needs *you.*

Chapter 9: Do Not Compare Yourself with Others – Overcoming Envy and Insecurity

The Trap of Comparison

"Do not compare yourself with others, for always there will be greater and lesser persons than yourself."

This line from *Desiderata* speaks directly to one of the greatest struggles of the human experience - comparison. We live in a world where success, beauty, wealth, and happiness are constantly measured against others. Social media, advertising, and societal expectations reinforce the idea that our worth is determined by how we stack up against those around us.

Comparison can be both inspiring and destructive. While seeing others succeed can motivate us to grow, it can also lead to envy, self-doubt, and dissatisfaction. The challenge is learning how to admire others without feeling inadequate, and how to pursue personal growth without measuring ourselves against someone else's journey.

This chapter explores why comparison is so deeply ingrained in human nature, how it affects our mental well-being, and practical strategies to break free from its grip.

Why We Compare Ourselves to Others

The tendency to compare is not entirely negative - it is a natural part of how humans understand their place in the world. However, unchecked comparison can become a source of insecurity and unhappiness.

1. Evolutionary and Social Conditioning

- Humans are wired for social comparison - it was a survival mechanism in early societies.

- In tribal communities, knowing one's status helped determine leadership, resource access, and group belonging.

- In modern life, this instinct remains, but it often manifests in unhealthy ways.

2. The Influence of Social Media and Culture

- We are constantly bombarded with images of "perfect" lives, curated to show only the best moments.

- Success is often defined by external markers - wealth, appearance, popularity, or achievements.

- This creates an illusion that others have it "better," leading to feelings of inadequacy.

3. The False Belief That Life Is a Competition

- Many people believe that success is a limited resource - that if someone else wins, they lose.

- In reality, success and happiness are not finite. One person's achievements do not diminish another's worth.

Comparison is inevitable, but when it becomes a source of self-doubt rather than motivation, it must be consciously managed.

The Negative Effects of Comparison

Unchecked comparison can have deep psychological and emotional consequences.

1. It Creates Insecurity and Self-Doubt

- Comparing our worst moments to someone else's highlights reel makes us feel like we are failing.

- Instead of appreciating our progress, we focus on what we lack.

2. It Destroys Gratitude and Contentment

- When we are constantly looking at what others have, we forget to appreciate what we already possess.

- Gratitude is replaced with a feeling of "never enough."

3. It Damages Relationships

- Envy can create resentment toward friends, colleagues, or family members.

- Instead of celebrating others' successes, we feel threatened by them.

4. It Leads to Unnecessary Stress and Anxiety

- The pressure to "keep up" leads to burnout and dissatisfaction.

- Instead of enjoying life, we constantly feel behind.

Comparison often leads to chasing goals that do not align with our true desires, simply because we feel we *should* achieve them. The solution is to shift focus from *others* to *ourselves*.

How to Stop Comparing Yourself to Others

Breaking free from comparison requires a conscious effort to reframe how we see success, happiness, and self-worth.

1. Focus on Your Own Journey

- Your life path is unique - comparing it to someone else's is like comparing a book in progress to a finished novel.

- Everyone moves at their own pace; success and happiness have no set timeline.

+ Reflect on this: Each time you feel the urge to compare, shift your focus to one thing you are proud of in your own life.

2. Limit Exposure to Comparison Triggers

- Social media can be a major source of unhealthy comparison.

- Unfollow accounts that make you feel inadequate and curate a digital space that uplifts you.

+ Reflect on this: Take a social media detox for a few days and observe how it affects your mindset.

3. Practice Gratitude Daily

- Gratitude shifts focus from what we *lack* to what we *have*.

- The more we appreciate our own blessings, the less we envy others.

+ Reflect on this: Each morning, write down three things you are grateful for about your own life.

4. Redefine Success on Your Own Terms

- Society may define success by wealth, status, or fame, but true success is personal fulfillment.

- Ask yourself: *What truly makes me happy? What do I value most?*

+ **Reflect on this:** Write your own definition of success and use it as your guide rather than external expectations.

5. Celebrate Others Without Feeling Less

- Someone else's success does not mean your failure.

- Learning to be genuinely happy for others creates a mindset of abundance.

+ **Reflect on this:** The next time you feel envy, reframe it as inspiration. Think, *If they can do it, so can I.*

Shifting from Comparison to Inspiration

Instead of allowing comparison to create envy, use it as motivation for growth.

1. Learn from Those Who Inspire You

- Instead of feeling intimidated by successful people, ask what lessons you can take from them.

- Success leaves clues - observe habits, mindsets, and strategies you can apply.

2. Use Comparison as a Tool for Self-Improvement

- If you admire something in someone else, ask how you can cultivate it in yourself.

- Instead of thinking, *They have what I don't,* reframe it as, *I can develop that skill too.*

3. Compete Only With Yourself

- The only real competition is between who you are today and who you were yesterday.

- Progress, not perfection, is the goal.

+ Reflect on this: Set personal milestones based on your growth, not someone else's achievements.

Conclusion: The Freedom of Self-Acceptance

"Do not compare yourself with others, for always there will be greater and lesser persons than yourself."

This wisdom from *Desiderata* reminds us that comparison is a never-ending cycle. No matter how much we achieve, there will always be someone who seems to have more. The key to happiness is not in chasing external validation, but in embracing our own path.

When we stop measuring ourselves against others, we gain:

+ **More confidence** in our unique journey.

+ **More gratitude** for what we already have.

+ **More peace** in knowing that we are enough as we are.

True success is not about being *better* than others - it is about being the best version of *yourself.*

So let go of comparison. Embrace your journey. And remember: the only person you need to be better than is the person you were yesterday.

Chapter 10: Nurture Strength of Spirit – Resilience in the Face of Hardship

The Inner Fortress: Building Resilience

"Nurture strength of spirit to shield you in sudden misfortune."

This wisdom from *Desiderata* speaks directly to one of the greatest truths of life: adversity is inevitable. No matter how carefully we plan, how hard we work, or how much we try to control our circumstances, there will be challenges - loss, failure, disappointment, uncertainty.

But while hardship is unavoidable, how we respond to it is within our power. Strength of spirit - resilience, courage, and inner fortitude - is what enables us to weather life's storms without breaking. It is not about avoiding difficulties, but about developing the capacity to rise above them.

This chapter explores the nature of resilience, why some people seem to withstand hardship better than others, and how we can actively cultivate spiritual strength to face life's uncertainties with grace and courage.

Understanding Resilience: Why Some People Bend, Not Break

Resilience is not just about surviving difficult situations - it is about growing from them. It is what allows some people to remain hopeful in the face of tragedy, to keep moving forward after failure, and to maintain peace even in uncertainty.

What Resilience Looks Like in Daily Life

+ **Bouncing back from failure** rather than giving up.

+ **Finding meaning in hardship** instead of feeling victimized.

+ **Remaining calm in uncertainty** rather than panicking.

+ **Keeping hope alive** even when circumstances seem bleak.

+ **Facing fear with courage** instead of letting it control you.

Resilient people are not immune to pain or fear - they simply refuse to let adversity define them.

The Components of Strength of Spirit

Resilience is not something we are born with - it is something we develop. Like a muscle, inner strength grows stronger with use. Here are the key components of a resilient spirit:

1. Mental Strength: The Power of Perspective

- Resilient people do not dwell on what they cannot control; they focus on what they can.

- They reframe challenges as opportunities for growth rather than insurmountable obstacles.

+ **Try this:** When facing difficulty, ask yourself, *What can I learn from this? How can I grow through this experience?*

2. Emotional Strength: Managing Stress and Fear

- Fear and stress are natural reactions to adversity, but resilience means not letting them take over.

- Learning to process emotions in healthy ways (journaling, meditation, talking to a trusted friend) builds emotional endurance.

✚ **Try this:** Instead of avoiding difficult emotions, acknowledge them. Say, *"I feel anxious right now, but I know this feeling will pass."*

3. Spiritual Strength: Faith, Purpose, and Meaning

- Whether through religion, philosophy, or personal belief, a sense of purpose helps people endure hardship.

- Spiritual strength comes from believing that life has meaning beyond momentary suffering.

✚ **Try this:** Reflect on your deeper purpose. What keeps you going even when things get tough?

4. Physical Strength: The Mind-Body Connection

- Taking care of the body (exercise, rest, nutrition) directly impacts mental resilience.

- A strong body supports a strong mind - physical activity is scientifically proven to reduce stress and boost mood.

✚ **Try this:** When feeling overwhelmed, move your body - go for a walk, stretch, or do deep breathing exercises.

How to Nurture Strength of Spirit

Building resilience is a lifelong practice, but there are specific steps we can take to cultivate inner strength.

1. Accept That Life Is Unpredictable

- Many people suffer because they resist change or expect life to be fair.

- Strength of spirit comes from accepting that uncertainty is part of existence.

+ **Try this:** When faced with change, remind yourself, *"I cannot control everything, but I can control how I respond."*

2. Develop a Growth Mindset

- Instead of seeing failure as an endpoint, view it as part of the learning process.

- People with a growth mindset see setbacks as stepping stones, not stop signs.

+ **Try this:** Next time something doesn't go as planned, ask, *"What can this teach me?"*

3. Practice Gratitude, Even in Hard Times

- Gratitude shifts focus from what is wrong to what is still good.

- Even in the darkest times, there is always something to be thankful for.

+ **Try this:** Each night, write down three things you are grateful for - especially on difficult days.

4. Surround Yourself with Supportive People

- Strength is not about facing everything alone - it is about knowing when to ask for help.

- A strong support system (family, friends, mentors) provides encouragement and perspective.

✚ Try this: If you are struggling, reach out to someone you trust instead of isolating yourself.

5. Cultivate Serenity Through Mindfulness

- Meditation, deep breathing, and time in nature help build resilience by grounding us in the present moment.

- When we are centered, external chaos has less power over us.

✚ Try this: Spend five minutes each morning in silence, simply breathing and centering yourself.

6. Strengthen Your Faith (Whatever That Means to You)

- Whether through religious faith, philosophy, or a deep belief in the resilience of the human spirit, having a guiding principle provides strength.

- Faith does not remove hardship - it gives us the courage to face it.

✚ Try this: Reflect on what gives your life meaning. Write it down as a reminder during difficult times.

Examples of Resilience in Action

History is filled with people who demonstrated incredible strength of spirit:

- **Nelson Mandela** – Imprisoned for 27 years but emerged without bitterness, leading South Africa to peace.

- **Malala Yousafzai** – Survived an assassination attempt and continued fighting for girls' education.

- **Viktor Frankl** – Holocaust survivor who found meaning in suffering, later writing *Man's Search for Meaning*.

These individuals faced unimaginable hardship, yet their spirit remained unbroken. Their stories remind us that human resilience is limitless.

Conclusion: Strength That Cannot Be Shaken

"Nurture strength of spirit to shield you in sudden misfortune."

This is not just advice - it is a call to prepare for life's uncertainties with courage and wisdom.

Hard times will come. Challenges will arise. But with inner strength, we can meet them not with fear, but with faith in our ability to endure.

By nurturing our resilience, we build a life where setbacks do not define us, where struggles do not break us, and where we move through life with the quiet confidence that we can withstand any storm.

True strength is not about avoiding hardship - it is about rising through it.

So take heart. You are stronger than you know. And no matter what life brings, your spirit has the power to rise above it.

Chapter 11: Many Fears Are Born of Fatigue and Loneliness – Overcoming Anxiety and Isolation

The Hidden Roots of Fear

"Many fears are born of fatigue and loneliness."

These words from *Desiderata* offer a deep insight into the nature of fear. We often think of fear as something external - threats, failures, or dangers that exist outside of us. But Ehrmann suggests that much of our fear is actually rooted in something internal: exhaustion and isolation.

When we are physically drained, mentally overwhelmed, or emotionally disconnected, our perception of the world changes. Small worries become overwhelming, doubts multiply, and we begin to imagine worst-case scenarios. Fatigue makes us feel weak, and loneliness makes us feel vulnerable. Together, they create the perfect storm for anxiety.

But just as these fears arise from within, so too can their solutions. This chapter explores how fatigue and loneliness contribute to fear, and practical ways to restore energy, connection, and serenity.

How Fatigue Amplifies Fear

When we are well-rested and balanced, we handle stress better. But when we are physically or emotionally exhausted, everything feels harder.

The Science of Exhaustion and Anxiety

- Lack of sleep increases the brain's **amygdala**, the part responsible for fear and stress responses.

- Fatigue reduces logical thinking, making us more reactive and emotional.

- When tired, we focus more on **threats** than **solutions**, leading to unnecessary fear.

Signs That Your Fear Is Rooted in Fatigue

✚ Worries seem bigger at night but feel less scary in the morning.

✚ You feel overwhelmed by small tasks that normally wouldn't bother you.

✚ You find it harder to control emotions or stay optimistic.

How to Reduce Fear by Overcoming Fatigue

1. **Prioritize Rest** – Sleep deprivation fuels anxiety. Create a healthy sleep routine.

2. **Take Breaks** – Mental exhaustion is as real as physical exhaustion. Step away when needed.

3. **Move Your Body** – Exercise boosts energy and reduces stress hormones.

4. **Eat and Hydrate Properly** – Blood sugar crashes and dehydration make anxiety worse.

5. **Slow Down** – If you're always rushing, your nervous system stays in stress mode.

Reflect on this: Next time you feel anxious, ask yourself, *Am I actually afraid, or just exhausted?* If it's fatigue, focus on rest first before making any big decisions.

How Loneliness Magnifies Fear

Humans are social creatures. Even the most independent people need connection. Loneliness not only creates emotional pain but also makes us feel more vulnerable to life's challenges.

The Psychological Effects of Loneliness

- Increases **negative self-talk**, leading to doubt and fear.

- Makes problems seem **bigger** because there's no one to give perspective.

- Weakens **resilience**, making it harder to bounce back from difficulties.

- Causes the brain to **overestimate threats** and **underestimate our ability to cope.**

Signs That Loneliness Is Fueling Your Fear

✚ You dwell on negative thoughts more when you're alone.

✚ You feel like your problems are worse than they actually are.

✚ You feel stuck in fear because there's no one to reassure you.

How to Reduce Fear by Overcoming Loneliness

1. **Reconnect with Others** – Reach out to a friend, even if just for a short chat.

2. **Find a Community** – Join a group, attend events, or engage in social activities.

3. **Express Yourself** – Talking about fears with someone can cut them in half.

4. **Help Someone Else** – Volunteering shifts focus from fear to purpose.

5. **Strengthen Your Relationship with Yourself** – Enjoy your own company through hobbies, journaling, or solo adventures.

Reflect on this: If you feel anxious, instead of isolating, connect with someone. A single conversation can completely shift your mood.

Breaking the Cycle of Fear, Fatigue, and Loneliness

1. Recognize the Pattern

Fatigue → Increased Stress → Loneliness → More Fear → More Exhaustion → Repeat.

✚ Awareness is the first step. When you feel overwhelmed, ask: *Am I actually in danger, or just tired and disconnected?*

2. Interrupt the Cycle

- **If exhausted** → Rest before making decisions.

- **If isolated** → Reach out to someone, even if it's just a text.

- **If overwhelmed** → Take a small action, instead of overthinking.

3. Build Daily Habits That Reduce Fear

- **Practice Mindfulness** – Stay present instead of worrying about "what ifs."

- **Limit Fear-Based Media** – News and social media amplify anxiety.

- **Focus on What You Can Control** – Fear thrives in uncertainty; take small steps forward.

Reflect on this: Next time fear arises, respond with self-care instead of panic. Sleep, connect, and breathe before assuming the worst.

Finding Peace in the Present Moment

"Many fears are born of fatigue and loneliness."

This simple truth reminds us that fear is often not reality - it is a product of how we feel in the moment. By nurturing our energy, maintaining connections, and grounding ourselves in the present, we reduce fear's power over us.

So when fear arises, pause. Take care of yourself. Reach out to someone. And remember: you are stronger than your worries, and you are never alone.

Chapter 12: You Are a Child of the Universe – Embracing Your Unique Purpose

Finding Your Place in the Universe

"You are a child of the universe no less than the trees and the stars; you have a right to be here."

These words from *Desiderata* are a profound affirmation of self-worth. They remind us that we are not insignificant, lost, or without purpose. Like the trees that grow without questioning their right to exist and the stars that shine without seeking permission, we, too, belong.

In a world where people often struggle with feelings of inadequacy, uncertainty, and self-doubt, this message is a call to embrace our existence with confidence. It invites us to recognize our unique purpose and to live with a sense of belonging in the vast, mysterious universe.

This chapter explores the meaning of this affirmation, why so many people feel disconnected from their purpose, and how we can fully embrace our rightful place in the world.

Why We Struggle to Believe We Belong

Even though we are part of the universe, many people feel like outsiders in their own lives. They struggle with questions like:

- *Do I really matter?*
- *What is my purpose?*
- *Am I enough?*

These doubts arise for several reasons:

1. A Society That Measures Worth by Achievement

- We are often taught that our value depends on success, productivity, or external validation.

- If we do not "achieve" enough, we may feel unworthy.

2. The Comparison Trap

- Social media and cultural pressures create unrealistic standards for what a "meaningful" life looks like.

- Instead of embracing our own journey, we compare ourselves to others.

3. Fear of Being "Not Enough"

- Many people believe they need to prove their worth - through relationships, careers, or external achievements.

- They forget that existence itself is enough.

But *Desiderata* reminds us that we do not need to *earn* our place in the world. We already belong.

Embracing Your Right to Be Here

The universe does not make mistakes. If you exist, it is because you are meant to.

1. Accept Yourself as You Are

- Trees do not apologize for growing; stars do not question if they should shine.

- You are enough simply by being.

+ **Try this:** Each morning, repeat the affirmation: *"I have a right to be here."*

2. Recognize Your Unique Contribution

- No one else has your exact experiences, thoughts, or talents.

- The world would be different without you.

+ **Try this:** Write down 5 things that make you uniquely *you.*

3. Stop Seeking Permission to Exist

- You do not need anyone's approval to take up space, follow your dreams, or be yourself.

- Your existence is already justified.

+ **Try this:** The next time you hesitate to express yourself, remind yourself: *"I am a child of the universe. I belong."*

Discovering Your Purpose

1. Purpose Is Not About Grand Achievements

- Many people think purpose means changing the world in a big way.

- But purpose can be found in small, everyday moments - kindness, creativity, connection.

2. Your Purpose Evolves Over Time

- You don't have to have everything figured out today.

- Your purpose will change and grow as you do.

3. Purpose Is Found in Being, Not Just Doing

- You do not need to "achieve" something to be valuable.

- Sometimes, your purpose is simply to exist, love, and experience life.

+ Try this: Instead of asking, *"What should I do with my life?"* ask, *"How can I be more present in my life?"*

The Universe Needs You Just as You Are

"You are a child of the universe no less than the trees and the stars; you have a right to be here."

This is your permission to stop doubting your worth. You are not here by accident. You do not need to prove yourself. You belong.

So take a deep breath, embrace your existence, and live with the quiet confidence that you are exactly where you are meant to be.

Chapter 13: With All Its Sham, Drudgery, and Broken Dreams, It Is Still a Beautiful World

Finding Beauty in Imperfection

"With all its sham, drudgery, and broken dreams, it is still a beautiful world."

These words from *Desiderata* acknowledge a truth we all face: life is not perfect. There is injustice, hardship, and disappointment. Dreams sometimes shatter. People let us down. Plans fail.

And yet, despite it all, the world remains beautiful.

This message invites us to hold two realities at once - to acknowledge life's pain without becoming consumed by it, and to embrace its beauty even in the midst of struggle. It is a call to resilience, to gratitude, and to seeing beyond the hardships to the goodness that still exists.

This chapter explores how to find beauty even when life feels difficult, how to shift our perspective from despair to hope, and how to cultivate a sense of wonder in a world that is both flawed and magnificent.

The Dual Nature of Life

Many people struggle to reconcile the beauty of life with its suffering. They wonder:

- *How can I see the world as beautiful when there is so much pain?*

- *How can I stay hopeful when bad things happen?*

- *How do I embrace joy without ignoring life's hardships?*

The answer lies in **acceptance** - understanding that both darkness and light exist, and that beauty does not require perfection.

Why Life Feels Difficult at Times

1. **Unrealistic Expectations**

    o   Many people believe life should be fair, predictable, or without suffering.

    o   When things go wrong, they feel betrayed, as if life has failed them.

2. **Focusing on the Negative**

    o   The human brain has a negativity bias - it naturally pays more attention to threats and struggles.

    o   This can make it easy to overlook life's beauty.

3. **Emotional Pain Feels Overwhelming**

    o   When we are hurting, it is hard to see the good around us.

    o   But even in pain, beauty still exists - we just have to look for it.

Life is not either *good* or *bad* - it is both. The challenge is learning how to find the good, even in difficult times.

How to Find Beauty in a Flawed World

1. Shift Your Perspective

-   Instead of focusing on what is missing, focus on what is present.

-   Beauty is not just in perfect moments - it is in simple things:

    o   A sunrise after a difficult night.

    o   The kindness of a stranger.

    o   Laughter in the midst of struggle.

+ **Try this:** Each day, find one beautiful thing, no matter how small. Write it down.

2. Accept That Suffering Is Part of Life

- Pain does not mean life is broken - it means life is real.

- Every hardship contains a lesson, a moment of growth, or an opportunity for change.

+ **Reflect on this:** Instead of asking, *"Why is this happening to me?"* ask, *"What can this teach me?"*

3. Practice Gratitude

- Even in difficult times, there is always something to be grateful for.

- Gratitude shifts the mind from despair to appreciation.

+ **Try this:** Before bed, list three things you are grateful for, even on hard days.

4. Seek Out Moments of Wonder

- Nature, music, art, and human connection remind us of life's beauty.

- When the world feels heavy, step outside - watch the sky, listen to birds, feel the wind.

+ **Reflect on this:** Set aside five minutes a day to simply observe something beautiful.

5. Choose to Believe in Goodness

- Despite pain, love exists.

- Despite corruption, kindness exists.

- Despite despair, hope exists.

+ **Try this:** When you feel overwhelmed by negativity, remind yourself: *Goodness is still here - I just have to notice it.*

The Strength to See Beauty in Hardship

Many of history's greatest figures found beauty even in suffering:

- **Anne Frank**, who, despite hiding from the horrors of war, wrote: *"I still believe, in spite of everything, that people are truly good at heart."*

- **Nelson Mandela**, who, after decades of imprisonment, chose forgiveness over bitterness.

- **Helen Keller**, who, despite being blind and deaf, found immense joy in life's small pleasures.

Their strength came not from denying pain, but from choosing to see beyond it.

Conclusion: Choosing to See the Beauty

"With all its sham, drudgery, and broken dreams, it is still a beautiful world."

Life will not always be easy. It will have heartbreak and challenges. But within the struggle, beauty remains. The sun still rises. Love still exists. Laughter still heals.

When faced with hardship, we have a choice: to focus on the darkness or to seek out the light. By choosing to see the beauty, we make life not just bearable - but truly meaningful.

So take a deep breath. Look around. The world is still beautiful, and so is your place in it.

Chapter 14: Be Cheerful, Strive to Be Happy – Living with Hope and Joy

The Choice to Embrace Joy

"Be cheerful. Strive to be happy."

These final words of *Desiderata* hold a simple yet profound truth: happiness is not something that just happens - it is something we cultivate. Life is filled with struggles, responsibilities, and unexpected difficulties, but within all of that, we still have the power to choose joy.

Happiness is not about ignoring problems or pretending that life is perfect. It is about cultivating a mindset that allows us to find light even in dark times. It is about recognizing that no matter what happens, we always have the ability to approach life with optimism, gratitude, and a sense of wonder.

In this chapter, we will explore what it truly means to "be cheerful" and "strive to be happy," the myths about happiness that keep us stuck, and practical ways to cultivate joy in daily life.

What Happiness Is - and What It Isn't

Many people chase happiness as if it is a final destination, believing that once they achieve a certain goal, they will finally feel fulfilled. But happiness is not a place - it is a way of traveling.

Common Myths About Happiness

1. **"I'll Be Happy When… (Success, Wealth, Love)"**

   o   Many people believe happiness is tied to external achievements: money, relationships, status.

   o   But happiness is not found *after* success - it is found *along the way*.

2. **"Some People Are Just Naturally Happier Than Others"**

   ○ While genetics play a role, studies show that much of happiness comes from habits, mindset, and daily choices.

   ○ This means happiness is something we can build.

3. **"Happiness Means Always Feeling Good"**

   ○ Being happy doesn't mean never feeling sad, angry, or frustrated.

   ○ True happiness includes resilience - the ability to experience emotions but not be controlled by them.

Happiness is not about avoiding difficulties - it is about learning to find joy *despite* them.

How to Cultivate Happiness in Daily Life

Happiness is a practice. By developing small habits and shifting our mindset, we can create a life that is filled with more joy, peace, and contentment.

1. Choose Gratitude Over Complaint

- The mind naturally focuses on problems, but we can train it to focus on blessings.

- Gratitude rewires the brain, making us happier over time.

  ✛ Try this: Each morning, write down three things you are grateful for.

2. Focus on What You Can Control

- Many people feel unhappy because they focus on things beyond their control.

- True happiness comes from directing energy toward what *can* be changed.

✚ **Try this:** When you feel stressed, ask, *"Is this within my control?"* If not, let it go.

3. Spend Time with Positive People

- Energy is contagious - surround yourself with those who uplift and inspire you.

- Let go of relationships that drain your happiness.

✚ **Try this:** Reach out to a friend who makes you feel good, even if just for a short conversation.

4. Find Joy in Small Moments

- Many people wait for "big" events to feel happy, but joy is found in everyday life.

- A good meal, a deep conversation, a sunset - these are the moments that create lasting happiness.

✚ **Try this:** At the end of each day, recall one small moment that brought you joy.

5. Laugh More, Worry Less

- Laughter is one of the quickest ways to shift your mood.

- It reduces stress, strengthens relationships, and increases resilience.

✚ **Try this:** Watch a funny movie, read something humorous, or spend time with people who make you laugh.

6. Give More Than You Take

- Helping others is one of the most powerful ways to boost happiness.

- Acts of kindness increase feelings of connection, purpose, and joy.

✚ **Try this:** Do one small act of kindness today, even if it's just a smile or a kind word.

7. Accept That Happiness Is an Ongoing Process

- There is no final moment where you will "arrive" at happiness - it is something you build every day.

- Even on hard days, you can find moments of light.

✚ **Try this:** Instead of chasing happiness, focus on *cultivating* it daily.

Happiness as a Choice, Not a Destination

Many of the happiest people in the world do not have perfect lives - they simply choose to focus on what brings them joy rather than what brings them down.

Consider individuals like:

- **The Dalai Lama**, who radiates joy despite years of exile and hardship.

- **Nelson Mandela**, who found hope even after decades of imprisonment.

- **Ordinary people**, who despite struggles, choose to wake up each day with gratitude and optimism.

Happiness is not about circumstances - it is about perspective.

Conclusion: Striving for a Joyful Life

"Be cheerful. Strive to be happy."

These words remind us that happiness is both an attitude and an effort. While we cannot control everything that happens in life, we can control how we respond to it.

Happiness is not about waiting for the perfect moment - it is about creating joy in the moments we have. It is about choosing gratitude over complaint, connection over isolation, and optimism over fear.

So wake up each day with the intention to find beauty, to smile more, to love more, and to live fully. Strive for happiness - not because life is perfect, but because you deserve to embrace its joy.

Final Thoughts: The Wisdom of *Desiderata*

As we come to the end of this reflection on *Desiderata*, we return to its central message:

- **Go placidly amid the noise and haste.**

- **Speak your truth with quiet confidence.**

- **Be kind to yourself and others.**

- **Let go of comparison, fear, and negativity.**

- **Trust that you belong, and that life - though imperfect - is still beautiful.**

These are not just poetic words - they are a guide for a life well-lived.

So take them with you. Carry them in your heart. And each day, choose to walk the path of peace, wisdom, and joy.

The world is still beautiful. You are still worthy. And happiness is always within reach.

Epilogue: Living the Wisdom of *Desiderata*

As we reach the end of this journey through *Desiderata*, we are reminded of the poem's quiet yet profound wisdom. In a world that often feels chaotic, overwhelming, and uncertain, *Desiderata* offers a steady guide - a philosophy for living with peace, integrity, and joy.

Its message is not about achieving perfection or escaping hardship but about navigating life with grace. It teaches us that:

- **Inner peace is possible, even amid noise and haste.**

- **Compassion - toward ourselves and others - creates a life of meaning.**

- **Authenticity and self-acceptance lead to freedom.**

- **Comparison and fear rob us of joy, but gratitude restores it.**

- **Resilience is the key to overcoming life's inevitable struggles.**

- **Despite all its imperfections, the world is still beautiful.**

Carrying *Desiderata* into Everyday Life

This book is not just meant to be read - it is meant to be lived. As you move forward, consider ways to integrate *Desiderata* into your daily life.

1. Start Each Day with a *Desiderata* Reminder

- Before the rush of daily life takes over, remind yourself of a single line from *Desiderata* to set the tone for the day.

+ **Example:** *"Go placidly amid the noise and haste."* – A reminder to stay calm, no matter what the day brings.

2. Use *Desiderata* as a Compass in Difficult Moments

- When faced with stress, conflict, or doubt, return to the poem's wisdom for guidance.

+ Example: *"Be yourself."* – A reminder to stay true to your values in difficult decisions.

3. Practice Gratitude and Perspective

- Even in hard times, remember the closing words:
  "With all its sham, drudgery, and broken dreams, it is still a beautiful world."

+ Try this: When overwhelmed, pause and list three things that are still good in your life.

4. Share the Wisdom with Others

- Just as *Desiderata* has inspired generations, pass its message along.
- Whether through kindness, encouragement, or simply living its principles, be a source of light in the lives of others.

+ Try this: Send a line from *Desiderata* to a friend who needs encouragement.

A Final Thought: You Are Enough, Just as You Are

Above all, *Desiderata* teaches us that we are enough. We do not need to prove our worth, seek endless validation, or wait for life to be perfect to embrace joy.

> You are a child of the universe. You belong here. And your life - though imperfect, filled with challenges and uncertainties - is still a beautiful journey.

> So go forward with peace in your heart, wisdom in your mind, and joy in your soul.

> Live fully. Love deeply. And always remember:

> *"Be cheerful. Strive to be happy."*

Thank You for This Journey

May the profound insight of *Desiderata* continue to guide you as you walk your unique path in life.

Bibliography

This book is inspired by *Desiderata*, the timeless poem by **Max Ehrmann**, and draws from various philosophical, psychological, and spiritual traditions to explore its wisdom in depth. The following sources were referenced, directly or indirectly, in shaping the insights and discussions within this book.

Primary Source

- Ehrmann, Max. *Desiderata*. 1927.

Books on Philosophy, Wisdom, and Mindfulness

- Aurelius, Marcus. *Meditations*. Translated by Gregory Hays, Modern Library, 2002.

- Carnegie, Dale. *How to Stop Worrying and Start Living*. Simon & Schuster, 1948.

- Frankl, Viktor E. *Man's Search for Meaning*. Beacon Press, 1946.

- Tolle, Eckhart. *The Power of Now: A Guide to Spiritual Enlightenment*. New World Library, 1997.

- Thich Nhat Hanh. *Peace Is Every Step: The Path of Mindfulness in Everyday Life*. Bantam, 1992.

- The Dalai Lama and Howard Cutler. *The Art of Happiness: A Handbook for Living*. Riverhead Books, 1998.

Psychology and Self-Development

- Brown, Brené. *The Gifts of Imperfection: Let Go of Who You Think You're Supposed to Be and Embrace Who You Are*. Hazelden Publishing, 2010.

- Clear, James. *Atomic Habits: An Easy & Proven Way to Build Good Habits & Break Bad Ones*. Avery, 2018.

- Dweck, Carol. *Mindset: The New Psychology of Success*. Ballantine Books, 2006.

- Goleman, Daniel. *Emotional Intelligence: Why It Can Matter More Than IQ*. Bantam, 1995.

Spirituality and Meaning

- Chopra, Deepak. *The Seven Spiritual Laws of Success: A Practical Guide to the Fulfillment of Your Dreams*. Amber-Allen Publishing, 1994.

- Lewis, C.S. *The Problem of Pain*. HarperOne, 1940.

- Rohr, Richard. *Falling Upward: A Spirituality for the Two Halves of Life*. Jossey-Bass, 2011.

- Sinek, Simon. *Start with Why: How Great Leaders Inspire Everyone to Take Action*. Portfolio, 2009.

Stoicism and Resilience

- Holiday, Ryan. *The Obstacle Is the Way: The Timeless Art of Turning Trials into Triumph*. Portfolio, 2014.

- Seneca. *Letters from a Stoic*. Translated by Robin Campbell, Penguin Classics, 1969.

- Stockdale, James B. *Courage Under Fire: Testing Epictetus's Doctrines in a Laboratory of Human Behavior*. Hoover Institution Press, 1993.

Modern Insights on Happiness and Well-Being

- Haidt, Jonathan. *The Happiness Hypothesis: Finding Modern Truth in Ancient Wisdom*. Basic Books, 2006.

- Lyubomirsky, Sonja. *The How of Happiness: A New Approach to Getting the Life You Want*. Penguin, 2007.

- Seligman, Martin. *Flourish: A Visionary New Understanding of Happiness and Well-Being*. Atria Books, 2011.

Articles and Studies on Mindfulness, Gratitude, and Mental Health

- Fredrickson, Barbara L. "The Role of Positive Emotions in Positive Psychology: The Broaden-and-Build Theory of Positive Emotions." *American Psychologist*, vol. 56, no. 3, 2001, pp. 218-226.

- Kabat-Zinn, Jon. "Mindfulness-Based Stress Reduction (MBSR) and Its Applications." *Clinical Psychology: Science and Practice*, vol. 10, no. 2, 2003, pp. 144-156.

- Kahneman, Daniel, and Deaton, Angus. "High Income Improves Evaluation of Life but Not Emotional Well-Being." *Proceedings of the National Academy of Sciences*, vol. 107, no. 38, 2010, pp. 16489-16493.

Inspirational Figures and Their Teachings

- Mandela, Nelson. *Long Walk to Freedom: The Autobiography of Nelson Mandela*. Little, Brown, 1994.

- Kahlo, Frida. *The Diary of Frida Kahlo: An Intimate Self-Portrait*. Abrams, 1998.

- Einstein, Albert. *Ideas and Opinions*. Crown Publishing, 1954.

Acknowledgment of Traditional Wisdom and Oral Teachings

This book also draws inspiration from various philosophical and spiritual traditions, including **Buddhism, Stoicism, Christianity, Sufism, and Indigenous wisdom**, which have long emphasized internal peace, resilience, and the interconnectedness of all things. While no single source captures these teachings fully, their influence is deeply woven into the reflections in this book.

Final Note on Sources

Many of the insights in this book are derived not only from published works but also from **personal experience, meditation, and reflection on life's journey**. As such, the profound insight of *Desiderata* continues to resonate across time, blending poetry with psychology, philosophy with everyday practice, and ancient truths with modern understanding.

Glossary

This glossary provides definitions and explanations of key terms, concepts, and philosophical ideas referenced throughout this book. These terms are drawn from *Desiderata* and related themes in mindfulness, psychology, and self-development.

A

- **Acceptance** – The practice of embracing reality as it is, without resistance or denial. Accepting both joy and suffering is a key to inner peace.

- **Authenticity** – The quality of being true to oneself, expressing thoughts, emotions, and values without pretense or fear of judgment.

- **Awareness** – A state of conscious presence, paying attention to thoughts, emotions, and surroundings without distraction or automatic reaction.

B

- **Balance** – A state of harmony between different aspects of life, such as work and rest, ambition and contentment, self-care and service to others.

- **Boundaries** – Emotional, mental, and physical limits that help protect personal well-being and maintain healthy relationships.

- **Burnout** – A state of emotional, physical, and mental exhaustion caused by prolonged stress, often due to overwork or a lack of self-care.

C

- **Comparison Trap** – The tendency to measure one's worth and success based on others, often leading to feelings of inadequacy or envy.

- **Compassion** – A deep awareness of others' suffering, accompanied by a desire to help or alleviate their pain. Compassion can be extended to oneself as well.

- **Confidence** – A sense of self-assurance and belief in one's abilities, independent of external validation.

- **Conscious Living** – A way of life in which actions, thoughts, and emotions are approached with awareness, intention, and mindfulness.

- **Contentment** – A feeling of satisfaction and peace with what one has, rather than constantly seeking more.

D

- **Desiderata** – Latin for "things desired" or "things needed"; the title of Max Ehrmann's poem, which serves as a guide to a peaceful, meaningful life.

- **Detachment** – The ability to let go of outcomes, possessions, or expectations without emotional suffering. Often linked to mindfulness and spiritual teachings.

- **Discernment** – The ability to judge wisely, especially in distinguishing truth from illusion, or ethical decisions from harmful ones.

- **Drudgery** – Tedious, repetitive, or unpleasant work that can feel exhausting but is often an unavoidable part of life.

E

- **Echo Chamber** – A social or media environment in which people are only exposed to opinions that reinforce their existing beliefs, limiting their perspective.

- **Empathy** – The ability to understand and share the feelings of another, fostering connection and compassion.

- **Ego** – The part of the self that seeks validation, recognition, and superiority over others; often a barrier to inner peace.

- **Emotional Intelligence** – The ability to recognize, understand, and manage one's emotions while also being aware of others' emotions.

- **Energy Drain** – A feeling of exhaustion caused by engaging with negative people, situations, or thoughts that deplete mental and emotional strength.

- **Ethical Success** – Achieving prosperity and fulfillment while maintaining integrity, honesty, and kindness in one's actions.

F

- **Fear-Based Thinking** – A mindset where decisions are driven by anxiety, insecurity, or worst-case scenarios rather than confidence and wisdom.

- **Flow State** – A mental state of complete immersion in an activity, characterized by focus, enjoyment, and the loss of self-consciousness.

- **Forgiveness** – The act of letting go of resentment toward oneself or others, not for the benefit of the offender but for inner peace.

- **Fulfillment** – A deep sense of satisfaction and purpose derived from meaningful work, relationships, and self-expression.

G

- **Gratitude** – The practice of recognizing and appreciating the good in life, which has been scientifically linked to increased happiness.

- **Growth Mindset** – The belief that abilities, intelligence, and character can develop over time through effort, learning, and perseverance.

- **Grounding** – The practice of connecting with the present moment through physical sensations, breath, or nature to reduce stress and anxiety.

H

- **Happiness Paradox** – The idea that chasing happiness directly often leads to disappointment, while focusing on purpose and gratitude naturally brings happiness.
- **Humility** – The quality of being humble, recognizing one's strengths and weaknesses without arrogance or self-deprecation.
- **Hope** – The belief in the possibility of a positive outcome, even in difficult times.

I

- **Impermanence** – The understanding that all things - good and bad - are temporary. A central concept in Buddhism and mindfulness practice.
- **Inner Peace** – A state of mental and emotional calm, free from worry, fear, and inner conflict.
- **Integrity** – The quality of being honest, ethical, and true to one's values, even when faced with challenges.
- **Intuition** – The deep, often subconscious knowledge or gut feeling that guides decision-making beyond logic.

J

- **Joyful Living** – A way of life that prioritizes happiness, appreciation, and presence rather than material success or external validation.
- **Judgment-Free Awareness** – Observing thoughts, feelings, or experiences without labeling them as "good" or "bad."

K

- **Kindness** – The act of treating others with compassion, understanding, and generosity, often with no expectation of return.
- **Karma** – The spiritual principle that one's actions influence future experiences, often associated with cause and effect in life.

L

- **Letting Go** – Releasing attachment to past hurts, expectations, or control over things beyond one's power.

- **Limiting Beliefs** – Negative thoughts or assumptions that restrict personal growth and confidence.

M

- **Mindfulness** – The practice of being fully present in the moment without distraction or judgment.

- **Minimalism** – A lifestyle that prioritizes simplicity, focusing on what truly adds value to life rather than accumulating excess.

- **Moral Courage** – The ability to stand by one's ethical principles even in the face of opposition or difficulty.

N

- **Negativity Bias** – The human tendency to focus more on negative experiences than positive ones, which can distort reality and increase stress.

- **Non-Attachment** – A practice of engaging with life fully while maintaining the ability to let go of expectations and outcomes.

O

- **Overthinking** – The tendency to analyze situations excessively, often leading to anxiety, indecision, and stress.

P

- **Perspective Shift** – The ability to change how one views a situation, transforming challenges into opportunities for growth.

- **Purpose** – A sense of meaning and direction in life, which can be found through relationships, creativity, work, or personal growth.

R

- **Resilience** – The ability to recover from setbacks, adapt to challenges, and keep moving forward with strength and optimism.

- **Restorative Practices** – Activities like meditation, nature walks, or creative expression that help restore mental and emotional balance.

S

- **Self-Compassion** – Treating oneself with the same kindness and understanding that one would offer a friend.

- **Serenity** – A state of inner calm, free from stress and agitation, often cultivated through mindfulness or spiritual practice.

T

- **Tranquility** – Deep peace and stillness, both internal and external.

W

- **Wisdom** – The ability to apply knowledge and experience with understanding, discernment, and compassion.

Final Thoughts

These concepts form the foundation of *Desiderata*'s message - guiding us toward a life of peace, resilience, and joy. By practicing these principles, we move closer to living with wisdom, kindness, and fulfillment.

www.ingramcontent.com/pod-product-compliance
Lightning Source LLC
Chambersburg PA
CBHW071614040426
42452CB00008B/1336